First Tracks

By Johnny Boyd

Illustrated by Jeff Teaford

FIRST TRACKS

Published by PTO Press – Peel the Onion
ISBN: 978-0-9760187-1-1   I   All rights reserved
Printed in the United States of America

Thanks to Patricia Logan, Ellie Roberts, Betsy Frank, Genevieve Smith, and Madeleine Osberger.
Extra special thanks to my wife Cassia for the layout and design, and for putting up with me while this project consumed my time.

Suzie Shane visits Yellowstone! Join her and the Shane family in The Yellowstone Kid.

TO ORDER BOOKS CONTACT:
ptopress@ptopress.com   I   www.ptopress.com

Follow us on Facebook PTO Press and Twitter@jb_ptopress

Though I mentioned a few of the front-line employees that our little guest might meet, this book is dedicated to all of the behind-the-scenes employees that make a ski resort function. You are the unsung heroes of the skiing world.

Hi there!
My name is Suzie Shane.
My family and I are going on an adventure.
We'll be riding on a plane.

4

We'll be flying somewhere far off.
Where it is I don't really know.
Daddy says there will be mountains and trees
and lots and lots of snow.

I'd like to bring some friends along
so you're invited, too!
Come with us on our vacation
and I'll show you what we do.

First you should meet my family.
I think they're pretty cool.
To go on this vacation
they took me out of school.

This is my Mommy and that's my Daddy
and here's my brother Jay.
Sometimes Jay is mean to me
but I love him anyway.

We've landed in the mountains where the air is crystal clear. The sky is so blue it's magical and over there's a deer!

We've checked into our hotel,
gone down to get some food.
Everyone is so nice here.
Not one person has been rude.

10

I'm going to try a sport called skiing
but I don't have all the facts.
Will someone be able to show me
how to make my very first tracks?

Before I can go outside to ski
I have to wear a real warm suit.
I'm as wide as I am tall
but Mommy says I'm cute.

Sure enough they have a way
to show me how to ski.
There's this place called ski school
and it's full of kids like me!

I have a nice instructor.
His name is Smilin' Jim.
He says to make my skis like a pizza
and then to follow him.

15

On my first run down the mountain
Oops! I take a fall
but I'm so close to the ground and the snow's so soft
it doesn't hurt at all.

While I'm lying on the ground
a man skis up like a breeze.
He pats the snow off of my coat
and lifts me to my skis.

16

He has a nice smile and a gleam in his eye.
He said he watched me roll.
"It's all part of learning to ski," he says.
This man is on ski patrol.

These ski patrol guys are awesome!
Seems like a sweet job to me.
They help people all day,
and they get paid to ski!

17

Now I get to ride the lift.
It goes high into the air.
I'm so far above the ground
I can see everywhere.

Riding the lift is kind of neat.
It's not that bad at all.
When I'm on the ground grown-ups are big.
From up here, they're small.

The lift comes to an end
and I go back downhill.
While riding the lift is fun,
the skiing is funner still.

Smilin' Jim knows a lot about skiing.
He seems oh-so-wise.
I think he's got a thing for food,
now he wants to make french fries.

Making fries means going fast
and going fast means fun.
It fulfills my need for speed
when I let my little skis run!

21

My second run I'm feeling brave,
so, I aim for a bump.
My skis fly up and off the snow.
Hey! I just did a jump!

I land my jump moving fast.
To slow down I make a turn.
My family will be so happy
when they see the things I've learned.

Jay decided not to ski;
he wants to snowboard instead.
He says that boarding is "way cooler,"
but I think that's all in his head.

Jay leans his board on one edge,
then he leans it on the other.
He shreds the mountain like a pro,
I'm so proud of my brother!

Snowboarding must be very fun
because it really makes Jay smile.
If he doesn't feel like bothering me,
then I'm a happy child!

25

My Mommy's an intermediate;
I don't know what that means.
She skis up on the blue runs,
while I stay down on greens.

My Daddy's been skiing a long time.
He makes it look so easy.
He skis on moguls and really steep stuff
that would make me feel queasy.

27

No matter how you go downhill
and no matter on what run,
be it on skis or snowboard
everyone has fun!

28

At the end of our skiing day
we take a shuttle to our hotel.
The drivers answer our questions.
They know this place so well.

These guys are my heroes.
They've treated me so nice.
They have a really important job
driving people home on ice.

We've had fun all week
but the time has come to go.
Daddy says we'll come back soon.
I really, really hope so!

I've had the best time on this vacation
and I hope you've enjoyed it, too.
The next time I go anywhere
if you can come, please do!

30

ABOUT THE AUTHOR

Johnny Boyd has spent the last 25 years working various jobs in ski resorts. His opinion column has appeared in the Snowmass Sun for the last 15 years and this is his third book. He lives in Snowmass Village, CO with his wife, Cassia.

ABOUT THE ILLUSTRATOR

Jeff Teaford has been drawing since childhood. His work can be seen on zillions of murals and artworks in the Roaring Fork Valley. He currently teaches children to ski for the Snowmass Ski School and lives in El Jebel, CO with his wife, Kim.